AF427938

by

Denise N. Fyffe

A Note to the Reader

Stealing is not only morally wrong, but also a criminal act; however, millions of workers are guilty of this crime. This issue is not aligned to only one nation or country, but it is a global pandemic, which must be obliterated.

Companies lose millions of dollars every year. Globally the losses total in the billions. With the advancement of technology, the sophistication of office thieves has only abounded beyond that of the law and judicial system.

This book will delve into theft and white-collar crime. It shall present strategies to deter office theft and finally present the findings from a study conducted at one Jamaican organisation.

-        *Denise N. Fyffe*

TABLE OF CONTENTS

PREFACE

It was the third time this month that Yvonne found something missing from her desk, her purse, or her bag. She was sick and tired of playing victim and suffering from this injustice. What could she do? There had been other thefts, and nothing came of it; the culprit was too smart, and management did not care about her missing stapler, tablet or $500. She did not know how long she could continue to work under such conditions, before blindly seeking revenge herself, while losing her moral compass. Something needed to be done; proper security measures need to be implemented so that she could leave her personal belongings at her desk and not worry when she went off to teach her classes. It was too burdensome to lug her handbag all over campus.

*****

Theft is a global problem costing business throughout the world billions of dollars every year. Employee theft is so devastating that numerous organisations have had to close their doors or even declare bankruptcy. Every year surveys and polls are conducted to examine just how much loss is experienced and to develop strategies that can minimise the occurrences of occupational theft. Businesses and workers are equally negatively impacted.

Workers are already faced with the challenge of completing their jobs successfully in any given day; it becomes even more difficult when they become distracted by security concerns. Employees should be able to leave their personal possessions at their desk, in a locker or at their station and return to find them undisturbed. This is not the case for many employees in Jamaica and unfortunately a pestering reality for a group of workers at one tertiary institution. This calls for proper strategies to be implemented to safeguard against repetitive future occurrences.

In this book, you will find an examination of employee theft from both the perspective of the business and the employee. Statistics and examples of employee theft and fraud will be presented. The true account will be discussed from all over the world including Australia, Ireland, the United States, the United Kingdom and especially Jamaica.

Afterwards the data collected from a study conducted at a multi-cultural tertiary organisation will be presented. It seeks to examine employee security concerns with a focus on theft, how frequently it occurs and then recommend strategies that can be implemented to deter future perpetrators of the act. A solid foundation would have already been laid in the examination and discussion of the occurrence of occupational theft within other industries. Then information will be given on the statistical findings of the informal survey conducted on workers at one of Jamaica's tertiary institutions. Finally, based on the results, recommendations will be proposed on how to address these security concerns at the institution.

THIEVES IN THE WORKPLACE

The Thief

Thieves are opportunists, whether they are amateurs or professionals. They endeavour to take advantage of any situation, which provides them a loophole. An opportunity to take what belongs to someone else. They are criminals who are indiscriminate and feel no immediate remorse when they hurt others. If the situation presents itself, a thief can get away with the act without much effort or planning because committing this type of crime is second nature to them.

A thief is even more likely to commit a crime when they are persuaded to do so; that is, when they have social, financial, or physical needs to be met. Financial obligations are always the main trigger. The influence of their peers or the desire to maintain their present lifestyle is others. The other factor is greed; wanting to have something that you desire at any cost. Most thieves are brought up in a culture of deviant or criminal behaviour, which is considered a subculture of their society.

Some persons look at stealing as a profession; it is a job where they spend time to refine the skills needed to maintain a constant level of success in their endeavours. They do not spend too long in one place. They are always scouting out new locations. They are precise and logical in their actions. Many are often charismatic and engage their victims without them becoming suspicious.

Other thieves are not so industrious; they do not hold this criminal act in such a high esteem. The amateur thief is more of an opportunist; he or she only engages in the activity when they are least likely to be caught. Some in this category simply do not put much preparation and thought into committing the crime. They are loners who learn more from their own successes and mistakes than from the tutelage of another.

It is not easy to pinpoint one category of people as being more likely to develop this criminal trait. Thieves are universal pariahs. Thieves are distinct as their motives differ. While one person might steal to meet everyday expenses, another might steal because it is a psychological addiction that can never be assuaged.

The Office Thief

Thieves in the workplace are not much different from those operating in other places. They are still opportunistic, but they have access to people who least would suspect them of such an offensive crime. It is often thought that those who commit office theft do so out of a feeling of dissatisfaction with their job or boss. Some thieves might feel exploited by their companies and wish to exact revenge by depriving the company of its assets, possessions, or secrets.

Criminality is not exclusive to the trenches of society; it has long existed in the corridors of the workplace. In this modern age, people who have this intent, find better ways of stealing secrets, depleting company resources and taking personal belongings of their fellow co-workers. Some culprits use the good reputation and office of their employers to enact fraudulent acts on the wider society. They lure them in and then misrepresenting themselves to gain thousands if not billions of dollars. It is important for businesses to note that most cases of employee theft are executed by long-term members of staff; those who seem dedicated to the business and have the trust of their employers.

Companies that wish to deter employee theft otherwise known as fraud, embezzlement, or occupational fraud, from happening against themselves and their employees must enforce strict moral and ethical codes of conduct. Each employee must have access to these codes and perpetrators who commit violations must be made an example of; no one likes embarrassment or to be disgraced publicly. However, whereas this is the utopia of expected industrial behaviour, it is not the regular modus operandi.

Many organisations are themselves guilty of mistreating their employees almost and over the point of it being a human rights violation; hence, they would never look out for the rights of their employees in any other way, at work. As such, they are more likely to look the other way or do nothing when an employee is the victim of office theft. Therefore, when you see lack of integrity, mistreatment, pressure, fraud, exploitation, low employee morale, low pay, purposeful frustration of the employee and rationalisation of a questionable act you will see that these organisations breed a culture of crime.

CHIEF EXECUTIVE OFFICER

White Collar Crime

The term 'white collar crime' or 'paper crime' is synonymous with these kinds of offences but committed by professionals who work in government or other industries. These criminals are often sophisticated cheaters, liars, and thieves. They leave behind numerous victims who are devastated and often cannot recuperate what they have lost.

It is said that poverty is the mother of crime and this statement can be deemed true even though there are those who have sufficient but are still greedy for more. However, with the increase in white-collar crime in Jamaica, one can see that there is a direct correlation to the high levels of poverty and deprivation currently affecting the country. People will become resourceful and create opportunities or means to take what rightly belong to others without earning it themselves. No place is it least expected but more rampant than in the workplace.

In the United States (US), companies overall lose upwards of US$50 billion annually due to employee theft. Jack L. Hayes International conducts a global Annual Retail Theft Survey of "23 of the country's largest retail companies with 18,900 stores and over $596 billion in 2012 retail sales. Just these 23 major retailers alone apprehended over 1.1 million shoplifters and dishonest employees and recovered more than $189 million from these thieves in 2012" (Lasky, 2013).

According to Fisher (2015), 43% of lost revenue at US retail companies can be attributed to their workers. That amounts to over US$18 billion, or US $2.3 billion more than that of shoplifters. "87% of occupational fraudsters had never been charged or convicted of a fraud-related offense, and 84%

had never been punished or terminated by an employer for fraud-related conduct "(Klein, 2014).

Occupational fraudsters who have worked for more than ten years at a company can defraud upwards of US$250,000 during their tenure while those working for under a year would embezzle a tenth of that amount. However, those in upper management are more likely to defraud their companies of larger amounts, even to the point where the business suffers major economic losses or shuts down.

Ireland is rated the highest for employee theft globally, with a loss of over €166 million Euros. This figure accounts for almost 37% of the overall shrinkage or loss of inventory experienced by retailers in that country. The Australian Police project that occupational fraud and theft caused businesses to lose $1.5 billion annually. The UK is not far behind with nearly $1.7 billion.

Globally, the occupational theft figure stands at nearly US$36 billion dollars, which is 28% of US$129 billion dollars of total lost experienced by retailers. This figure is derived from the annual survey conducted by an organisation called the Global Retail Theft Barometer. They surveyed retailers from 24 countries spanning Asia Pacific, Europe, and America. Below you can see the percentage of loss attributed to employee theft by country:

- United Kingdom – 33%

- United States - 32%

- Argentina – 15%

- Australia – 27%

- Belgium – 28%

- Brazil - 26%

- China – 35%

- France – 22%

- Germany – 24%

- Hong Kong – 22%

- Italy - 27%

- Japan - 31%

- Mexico - 37%

- Netherlands – 19%

- Portugal – 30%

- Spain - 27%

In Jamaica, there have been several high-profile cases of non-violet thieves operating in the workplace. In 2005, there was a reported case of a woman working for the Passport Office who stole over 700 passports, which she charged people more than $27,000 per passport. She was apprehended by the fraud squad for defrauding clients and her company of more than $18,900,000. Her crimes included larceny, forgery, uttering forged documents, conspiracy to deceive and breaches of the Corruption Prevention Act.

In 2012, the Postmaster General and Auditor General's Department in Jamaica identified that over $5 million dollars has been stolen or defrauded in recent years. It seems employees converted US money orders through fraudulent means. Also in 2012, a major discovery was made by the Department of Correctional Services where perpetrators stole the identifications of some of the employees. The guilty party retrieved the voters' ID and TRN card information to create, fraudulently, fake identification. While conducting the audit further white-collar crime activities were discovered. "It appears to be an elaborate identity-theft scheme involving fraudulent taxpayer registration numbers (TRN) and fake voters' identification cards in the name of employees. Some of the DCS employees have also been caught in the audit. The use of doctored payslips, boasting inflated net-pay figures, was identified by the auditors. It was clear that some employees had been falsifying salary figures on their payslips to qualify for loans from financial institutions that would otherwise be above their pay grade" (Reid, 2012).

No one seems to be above committing fraudulent activities as the same people put in positions to defend the rules and law of the land, are also engaging in white-collar crime. In 2015, a lawyer was convicted of fraud after she failed to pay over the motor vehicle settlement won for her clients. In that same week, another attorney was arrested and charged with forgery and conspiracy to defraud. There are two other cases presently in the courts against lawyers who have defrauded millions from their clients.

The Jamaica Constabulary Force Fraud Squad has been working assiduously to rectify the increasing number of fraud cases, which are specific to financial crime. 2007 saw 498 cases being reported or a loss of J$218 million, US$781,000 and £8,500 as opposed to 796 cases in 2008. As a direct result of employee theft, companies lost J$63 million. In 2012, the total defrauded figure for reported cases was approximately $1.5 billion Jamaican dollars and US$6 million (over J$600 million). "In 2010, there were 549 reported cases of fraud. By 2011, there were 574 reported cases. For the first quarter of 2012, there are 141 reported cases" (Helps,

2012); as of 2015, the overall amount was J$2.15 billion over three years.

These examples clearly indicate that thieves are as prevalent in the Jamaican workplace as anywhere else in the world. Due to the lack of stringent regulations, laws, and resources to catch the perpetrators early, these acts are repeated on numerous occasions before by the same criminals. However, whereas the criminals previously mentioned operate at a higher level, there are those who commit petty criminal acts that still affect employees adversely.

Office Theft

Victims of office theft are often left feeling angry, frustrated, and disappointed. It is too common an experience and it is not a problem that is impossible to resolve; companies simply need to commit to implement proper security measures, which make it difficult for thievery to thrive. Far too many employees can identify with the predicament of having had some small but significant item stolen from their desks, trays, drawers, filing cabinets and office fridge. From thousands of dollars, folders with information or even technological devices such as jump drives, tablets and compact disks, items continuously go missing. The victims rarely report the matter, as they are faced with the ever present and reoccurring answer that nothing can be done about it; as a result, they experience the effects of 'job withdrawal syndrome'. This includes de-motivation, anger, impatience, and overall job dissatisfaction. The victims of office theft are simply fed up.

Like the flu, office theft seems to continue unabated. Nevertheless, employees who are directly affected are the ones who must use their initiative to lobby for changes within their organisation. The perpetrator of these acts is safe and reassured each time, as he/she experiences a 'junkie's high' and adrenaline rush, though leaving them with an incurable appetite for more. Like any addict he/she must be cut-off from their supplier and strongly deterred from stealing again. To further understand office or employee theft, a variety of articles and sources have been chosen, which gives insight into this recurring and emerging phenomenon within the offices of Jamaican institutions.

Office theft is an obvious disregard of the eighth commandment given by God in the book of Exodus, where it states, "thou shall not steal" and also combined in the tenth commandment of not to "covet anything that is your neighbour's". However, according to the American Heritage®

Dictionary theft is defined as "the act or an instance of stealing; larceny." In addition, the legal definition states that a theft is a serious crime, like murder, that is punishable by more than one year of imprisonment; it is the taking of someone else's property with the intention of permanently depriving that person of it.

There are various types of office theft where employees either steal money, time, supplies, company property or information. The most common item in this category is money but currently of technological advancement, trade secrets are ranking high on the list as well. The other longstanding area of theft would relate to company time and fraudulent workers' compensation claims; this can present itself when employees try to misappropriate company time by taking unauthorized leave. Items that are frequently stolen include, "co-workers' belongings, computer or phone equipment, office décor (including paintings and plants), coffee packets, tea bags and condiments, toilet paper, band-aids, confidential files and copying, faxing, or shipping services for personal use" (Careerbuilder.com, 2007).

"A 1997 study conducted by American Society for Industrial Security (ASIS) discusses intellectual property theft, including the bootleg copying of compact discs, computer programs, books and other products covered by copyright or trademark laws. Survey statistics reveal that $44 billion worth of these products were targeted in a 17-month period. All U.S. companies could continue to lose more than $250 billion annually from this crime alone" (Stirn, 2014).

Office theft is a worldwide problem and Stirn (2014) points out that the U.S

Chamber of Commerce estimates that theft by employees cost American companies $20 billion to $40 billion a year. To pay for it, every man and woman working in America …contributes more than $400 per year. Also 75% of employee-related crimes go unnoticed."

No one is exempt from being a suspect. Jacoby (1999), quoting Michael Kessler, president, and chief executive of Michael G. Kessler & Associates states that "it goes all the way to the top from corporate vice presidents to janitorial staff". It is essential to note that some employees walk out in plain sight with stolen items. "Nearly every business experiences some degree of employee theft. Nearly one-third of all bankruptcies are caused by employee theft. However, less than 10% of the employee population is responsible for more than 95%

of the total losses from employee theft. "Although workplace theft is probably somewhat more widespread among blue collar workers, the damage done by more senior employees is usually far greater" (Jacoby, 1999). In addition, the Wall Street Journal reported that up to 75% of all employees steal at least once, half of these, at least twice. The Federal Bureau of Investigations in the United States believes that employee theft is the fastest growing crime in that country. All types of people commit office theft, and many this act goes unnoticed by companies.

Careerbuilder.com posted on their website the findings of its survey conducted on managers in June 2006 of 2,200 workers including 1,000 managers and discovered noteworthy facts. "Although only one-in-ten workers admitted to stealing from their employers, 38 percent of hiring managers reported they have fired employees for office theft. Office supplies topped the list of hot loot with 15% of hiring managers stating employees were most often caught red-handed with these items. Money came in second at 14% and merchandise placed third at 11%. Break rooms, co-workers' cubicles and even the first aid kit were also designated targets for theft."

Employee theft is committed for various reasons. "Whether it is worker dissatisfaction, a sense of entitlement, the thrill of the steal or some other reason, this behaviour communicates a lack of shared values with the company." Bacas (1987), quoting psychologist William Terris, states that "most thefts are never detected, and those that are detected are probably not representative of theft in general. Three factors affect whether an individual employee steals personal integrity, situational pressures, and opportunity. Does the person lack basic honesty: Is he or she predisposed to steal? Has the person incurred heavy debts or financial losses? Does the person seek revenge against the employer? Does he or she see peers stealing? Does the person handle money or goods without supervision? Are company accounting controls weak?"

The consequences vary for office theft. Taylor (2006), quoting from the June 2006 survey conducted by Careerbuilder.com outs forward that "45% of hiring managers would automatically fire someone discovered stealing, while 7% would not fire the thief. Some 48% of hiring managers said they did not have a clear-cut policy regarding employee theft and would decide whether or not to fire an employee caught stealing based on the object stolen and the situation."

Types of theft

Employers should be extra vigilant when it comes to these kinds of frauds:

- Accounting systems
- Accounts payable
- Banking systems
- Company accounts
- Computer systems
- Credit cards
- Fake or foreign orders
- Forged invoicing
- Inventory

- Kickbacks
- Payroll systems
  - Falsified work hours claim
- Petty cash
- POS and credit systems
- Royalty payments
- Sales commissions
- Travel expenses

Absenteeism as a form of Office Theft

Absenteeism can be defined as the "habitual failure to appear, especially for work or other regular duty" or "the rate of occurrence of habitual absence from work or duty." This definition is proposed by the American Heritage Dictionary. It is one of the most persistent obstacles to productivity, profitability, and competitiveness. It causes overtime, late deliveries, dissatisfied customers, and a decline in employee morale amongst workers who are expected to cover for an absent employee. The indirect costs often exceed the direct cost of absenteeism.

Many employees are guilty of this act, especially as they do not report the days, they are absent so that it can be deducted from their salaries. There are two types of absenteeism, innocent absenteeism, and culpable absenteeism. "Innocent absenteeism refers to employees who are absent for reasons beyond their control, like sickness and injury. Innocent absenteeism is not culpable which means that it is blameless. In a labour relations context this means that it cannot be remedied or treated by disciplinary measures. Culpable absenteeism refers to employees who are absent without authorization for reasons which are within their control. For instance, an employee who is on sick leave even though they are not sick, and it can be proven; this person is guilty of culpable absenteeism. To be culpable is to be blameworthy. In a labour relations context this means that progressive discipline can be applied."

Strategies to deter workplace theft

It is in the best interest of companies that they implement a plethora of strategies to deter not only white-collar crime but also simple office theft. Considering the statistics from the Fraud Squad, it is apparent that in Jamaica billions of dollars are lost. However, on a global scale companies have been shut down due to this kind of crime.

The buy in must take place at the management level and then the security strategies will trickle down throughout the organisation. The implementation must be comprehensive; else, perpetrators will find the areas of least resistance, the gaps. Strategies may be as simplistic as paying employees fairer wages to performing frequent audits, risk analyses, screening, and employee training on the matter.

Companies should never seek to protect only their reputation and not report criminal offences; simply firing someone leaves them to go somewhere else and enact the same crime. Management or victims must call in law enforcement officers, the Fraud Squad, or officers from local police stations, to handle the situation while equally protecting the rights of the victims and offenders.

Better Wages and Benefits

Office theft can be eliminated or minimised through various measures. According to Taylor (2006), "providing employees with adequate compensation and improving morale can also remove the incentive to steal. Employees steal from the companies they work for because they feel the company owes them. Either because they are underpaid, underappreciated or simply disengaged from mission of the company and have no personal stake in its success." Henry (1997) "urges training of all employees in theft technique recognition — even the thieves. The dishonest employees will realize they might be caught by another employee and decide to seek other employment where the risk is less."

JE 518
DOLLARS
20 EURO
10 EURO
EURO
EURO
JE 518175339 A
D 561802056
JE 518175533 A
500 EURO
500 EURO

Employee-Assistance Program

Fenn (1995) recommends an employee-assistance program. "Greed is a chief motivator, but financial difficulties, substance abuse and even mental-health problems can also lead to theft. Provide a problem-solving forum for your workers and you may be helping to defuse their impulse to steal." He further suggests establishing checks and balances, controlling inventory and to educate employees. Management can educate employees by "showing them how bottom-line repercussions of theft affect the company and encourage their help. Outline procedures for reporting theft, ensure confidentiality and lay out the consequences of dishonesty."

Joe Roche also recommends utilising Employee Assistance Programs (EAPs), in his article on CareerJournal.com the Wall Street Journal. It states that EAPs, "with their focus on early intervention, have a proven record for efficiency and cost-effectiveness. The concept is simple. Give workers convenient access to no-cost short term counselling and employers also reap the benefit: an increase in productivity, employee satisfaction and supervisor effectiveness and a decrease in absenteeism/presenteeism, health care costs and employee turnover."

Incentive programs

Lee (2000) believes that incentive programs improve office morale. He posits that they do not need to be well planned and should incorporate rewarding workers for accomplishing the company's objectives and team goals. He also points out that reward programmes can start small. One needs to "be creative with rewards. You don't have to offer the traditional trophy or plaque."

Integrity Tests

"Honesty tests, also called integrity tests, evaluate an individual's attitudes towards theft and other wrongdoing; although the terms honesty and integrity are generally interchangeable." These tests "attempt to evaluate an individual's attitudes towards theft and other wrongdoing through a series of questions." They highlighted four categories in which these questions would fall. They are "the admission of illegal or unacceptable activities such as having engaged in theft, criminal activity and/or drug use; the test takers' opinions toward illegal or inappropriate activities; the test takers' descriptions of his/her own personality or beliefs and an individual's reactions to theoretical and/or hypothetical situations. To predict future dishonest behaviour, honesty tests are most often used as a pre-employment tool to identify and to screen out individuals who are most likely to steal and/or be dishonest" (Eisenberg and Johnson, 2001).

In relation to honesty tests, employees are most times reluctant to disclose whether they have stolen in the past and may not disclose this information in the interview. Capell (2007) discusses the reluctance, and the dilemma employees face whether to disclose prior theft. Many employees would not divulge such information and are concerned "if you do disclose it, will it harm your job." Some believe that being upfront about the issue is better than the company finding out and the individual being dismissed.

Antitheft Policy

Bacas (1987) recommends that companies formulate and publish an antitheft policy. Jacoby (1999) states, that "audio and video surveillance is ineffective, as thieves can stay out of their range." Having surveillance also causes workplace tension. He suggests a business-friendly approach. "Pre-employment screenings can be an effective deterrent. They might reveal whether a job seeker was fired for stealing at a previous place of employment or whether someone otherwise lied on his or her application." During the process "employees should be screened for trustworthiness and this can be carried out through written pre-employment honesty tests; if used properly, it can pinpoint a potential or actual thief" (Bacas, 1987). Security audits are also helpful as they allow employers to identify problems early.

Physical Security

Physical security is also important in decreasing the likelihood of people stealing from companies, especially in retail businesses where stock is readily accessible by bought customers and workers. Where there is an abundance of control systems like cameras, CCTVs, safes, access control systems, gates and fences, motion detection systems, security personnel posts etc.; there will be minimal occurrences of office theft. Signs should be posted to notify employees and visitors of the purpose of these instruments and the outcomes if anyone are caught committing a crime.

THE STUDY

An examination of the security concerns of employees in an urban multi-disciplinary tertiary institution in Jamaica

Workers and by extension their job satisfaction experienced at the organisation is generally affected by problems such as theft and the implications of such are far reaching. If this problem continues then the Jamaican organisation will lose valuable employees who prefer to operate in an environment where they feel secure and have fewer or no worries about the security of their personal and work items. Upon this basis an examination of the security concerns of employees in a multi-disciplinary tertiary institution in Jamaica was done.

The research sought to determine the frequency by which security breaches or office theft occurred and then to make recommendations on how to resolve this issue. It also sought to identify the variety of items stolen and the area where this occurrence is most frequent. From this research other sub questions are derived which are an amalgamation of ingredients to produce an improved comprehension of this recurring problem. These questions include: How does one prevent the issues experienced by workers, which derive from such a problem? What measures can be implemented to address this problem? How does one address security violations?

Limitations existed that affected the outcome of this study. The first limitation was the difficulty arose in locating persons who were willing to participate in the research, as persons were generally suspicious of its true purpose. In keeping with good research practices, I readily admit that there were flaws with the research instrument, the questionnaire. Even though a pre-test was conducted, it became obvious that a few of the instructions were either ambiguous or not properly written. Examples can be seen at questions one and three where the instructions were not quite straightforward. For some questions, multiple responses were given, as there was no indication whether to select one as opposed to two or more options. The responses will invariably affect the implications and recommendations given from this study.

Findings

This section is deemed one of the most important of the study. The data collected is represented using bar and column graphs, along with pie charts. Using legends X and Y scales, the tallies and percentages will be shown. Several key questions from section A of our questionnaire will be individually represented. Section B is represented with a collective graph and a chart depicting the overall responses to the section and Section C is similarly represented. These charts can be referred to in the appendices.

The pie chart in Figure 1.0 shows the percentage of respondents who think their organisation is secure. Seventy six percent of the total respondents do not think the organisation is secure. However, 24% agrees that the organisation is secure. The diagram is proportioned to represent these facts.

Figure 2.0 shows that majority of the respondents have experienced a security breach at this Jamaican organisation. This majority is 81% of the respondents versus 19% of the persons.

The bar graph in Figure 3.0 is a pictorial representation of the responses chosen to represent the items that have been stolen. It is not reflective of the total number of participants as four have given more than one response to this question and two had no responses. However, of the 13 respondents that did not give varying responses, money received the highest of five responses. Cell phones, and jump drives had equal responses.

Seven respondents indicated that they did not report any breach while another six indicated that they have reported incidents of office theft. Four respondents did not respond. This is depicted in Figure 4.0.

Overall, 59% of the respondents indicated their disagreement that this Jamaican organisation's policy on security was clearly communicated. Eighteen percent completely disagreed, correspondingly another 12% agreed with the statement. Twenty nine percent were undecided.

In Figure 6.0, 70% versus 12% of the respondents disagreed that adequate measures were in place to address security.

Eighteen percent were undecided. Figure 7.0 represents the pie chart 'I feel more secure in my working environment'. Sixty two percent of the respondents disagreed with this statement. Only 19% agreed while another 19% were undecided.

Six percent of the respondents did not indicate a response for this statement; however, of the remaining 92%, 64% were dissatisfied with the strategies implemented to deal with security breaches. Another 6% were satisfied but 24% remained neutral.

Twenty four percent of the workers were neutral about their job satisfaction. In Figure 9.0, 35% were satisfied, however 31% had some level of dissatisfaction with this Jamaican organisation. None of the respondents was very satisfied with their job.

Analysis and Discussion

The analysis and discussion of the data collected will be presented by performing a separate examination on each section of the questionnaire and an inference along with the comparisons made to the literature review outlined.

Of the 20 questionnaires distributed and administered, only 17 were returned. The population was 17 females. These persons were equally representative of the persons who were directly affected by security breaches, in various departments of the organisation. While this may not be representative of an actual equitable distribution, it is believed to be an adequate sample. A 76% majority do not think that the organisation is secure. When asked to indicate why, the responses varied. However, employees indicated that they were not secure because items were stolen on a weekly basis, persons have access to your personal belongings and others are able to access staff without being questioned while security guards are not strategically placed on the compound.

Eighty one percent of the employees indicated that they have experienced various security breaches. Only two employees said they have not had this happen to them, but they knew of instances of office theft experienced by their fellow colleagues. Of the 81% of our respondents who participated, 15% said breaches occurred two years before. Another 15% of the persons working at this Jamaican organisation indicated that breaches occurred one year before, 37% said that breaches occurred in the recent weeks and months while 23% did not indicate a response.

Of the number of items stolen, most persons indicated that money was taken more frequently. For thirty-one percent of the time that money went missing, while cell phones and jump drives tied for 13%. Of the 17 responses, five indicated money taken from $500 to $3000 Jamaican and United States currency was stolen as well. This concurs with the Stirn's (2007) data, which clearly states that items that are frequently stolen include, "co-workers' belongings, computer or phone equipment".

Forty one percent of the workers indicated that they did not report the offense because in the past others or themselves have received no restitution; only 35% reported the incidents. Of the six respondents who did report the issue, two persons indicated that, in a span of two years that the perpetrators were dismissed. One worker of this Jamaican organisation stated that they had to replace the item stolen and only received sympathy, while the other member of staff indicated that nothing was done. Eighty percent of the employees clearly stipulated that they believed nothing would be done.

Section B was one of the critical areas of the questionnaire as it asked for the respondent's agreement to several key areas to the research topic, one of which is whether the company clearly communicates its security strategies. Fifty nine percent of the respondents were not in favourable agreement to the communication of security strategies and that adequate measures are in place to address security and safety issues; only 12% agreed. This is an indication that this multi-disciplinary tertiary institution should not only clearly communicate these policies, but also new strategies need to be developed and implemented. Sixty two percent of their employees do not feel secure in the working environment. Only two (2) respondents agreed that they felt secure. Twice as many persons were dissatisfied than satisfied about either the plans being implemented or resulting job satisfaction and as many employees remained neutral on the issue.

Workers were asked to indicate comments or suggestions to handle security issues and 46% of which gave some suggestions. They clearly indicated that they did not know the company's policies. One respondent suggested that security cameras be installed, especially in areas where there is a high level of breaches. Jacoby (1999) statements disagree with this as "audio and video surveillance are ineffective, as thieves can stay out of their range." Having surveillance also causes workplace tension. He suggests a business-friendly approach. Another respondent recommended that security be posted at strategic locations and have more patrols of not only the grounds but the offices as well. Several respondents were concerned that visitors and students had easy access to areas where the staff had their personal belongings. One suggestion was that there should be an area for greeting and interacting with students and visitors.

The researcher has observed instances of employee dissatisfaction at this multi-disciplinary tertiary institution. Staff members were openly disgruntled about the occurrence of theft in the offices and clearly communicated that the strategies to handle the issue was not effective. Employees openly expressed that the directive given by management was unreasonable. It was not feasible to carry your personal belongings and not leave them unattended in the offices. Most employees were lecturers and could not be expected to implement this request. Administrative staff had the same sentiments as well.

Employees indicated that the only obvious recourse was sympathy and therefore they saw no need to report theft as nothing would be done. Through an informal interview, management in its defence stated that little could be done, except to install security cameras and this would pose other problems. The central administration upon a direct complaint checked the doors and office drawers for functionality and distributed keys. However, this was no deterrent as office theft continued.

Implications

To this point, in the examination of security concerns of employees in an urban multi-disciplinary tertiary institution in Jamaica, we have reviewed articles written by several writers; this adds a level of credibility to the research conducted. Further, the data collected from the survey has been presented; results and observations were collated from both the quantitative and qualitative methods used. A presentation of the results was done following analyse and discussion. This related them to the arguments posited from other sources.

Now, in analysing the data collected from this research the quality of responses to the questionnaire is satisfactory. These responses have invariably affected the recommendations given from this study. Seeking to provide implications derived from the three sections of the questionnaire and promptly addressing several of the key areas, recommendations will be given on how to address security breaches and how best to implement these strategies and measure the effectiveness.

Recommendations

There are recommendations, which have been generated from the questionnaire responses or the lack thereof, as well as from the researcher's observation.

Recommendations being pro-offered:

- The management of this urban multi-disciplinary tertiary institution in Jamaica needs to communicate clearly and repeatedly the strategies and policies for security and safety.

- From the statistics more persons were dissatisfied than those satisfied with security policies. Therefore, the organisation needs to create room for improvement in these areas.

- Increase the presence and visibility in office areas of the security personnel.

- Managers and supervisors should receive training on how to handle security breaches and how to respond to victims.

- For all levels and classification of staff, provide employees with adequate compensation improving morale to prevent any desire or opportunity for security breaches.

- Outline procedures for reporting theft, ensure confidentiality and lay out the consequences of dishonesty.

- Implement honesty tests or integrity tests, to evaluate an individual's attitude towards theft and other wrongdoing.

- Formulate and publish an antitheft policy

The organisation needs to communicate clearly and repeatedly the strategies and policies for security and safety. Employees are of the impression that nothing is being done to address the issue of theft.

Therefore, with continued communication of these strategies staff can be reassured that their concerns are being addressed; thereby decreasing the levels of dissatisfaction. This can be done using the 'webmail' system or periodic letters.

From the statistics more persons were dissatisfied than those satisfied with security policies. These strategies can be improved, through an increased presence and visibility in office areas of the security personnel, or procedures implement to prevent unauthorised personnel or students from accessing staff rooms. Common areas can be created where students can meet with staff. Students would not be allowed to walk directly into areas of the registry without the persons being visited being at their desk or granting access. Auxiliary members should be accompanied by supervisor or security personnel who will take direct responsibility or accountability if any breach occurs.

Managers and supervisors at this urban multi-disciplinary tertiary institution in Jamaica should receive training on how to handle security breaches and how to respond to victims. Persons who have experienced security breaches are often upset and angry. The last reaction they need from management is sympathy. These workers want to hear that something will be done to address their problems and that something will be done. Managers need to be educated on how to deal with these employees without making the situation worse.

For all levels and classification of staff, provide employees with adequate compensation improving morale to prevent any desire or opportunity for security breaches. It has been stated when reviewing other writings that employees who are disgruntled and receive low pay are more likely to steal. When they are compensated adequately and fairly, they are less likely to breach security. Rewards and incentive schemes for outstanding job performance can also keep employees happy and morale high. Incentive schemes are normally accessed by the general and administrative staff; however, this should be granted to auxiliary staff as well.

Management should outline procedures for reporting theft, ensure confidentiality and lay out the consequences of dishonesty. Policies and procedural documents should be distributed and displayed in key locations for any staff member to access. These policies should also be discussed with new employees by supervisors. During annual or the quarterly period, they should be reiterated to employees. A forum should be in place for these procedures to be improved or adjusted as the need arises.

Honesty tests or integrity tests should be utilised by hiring managers to evaluate an individual's attitude towards theft and other wrongdoing. This should be incorporated in the interview process. According to Bacas (1987), these tests act as an effective deterrent. "They might reveal whether a job seeker was fired for stealing at a previous place of employment or whether someone otherwise lied on his or her application." Honesty tests are a preventive measure. They will help to ensure less security breaches in the organisation.

Conclusion

Office theft can be seen as an unwelcome guest at a lavish dinner party, where the hosts are ashamed to acknowledge its existence in their home. But how do the guests feel about staying throughout the party or even returning for another such event. Would security not be the number one factor on their minds? Would this blemish not be the inauspicious topic at the water coolers and bedsides of workers? Is this something the host really wants to ignore? Or pray would leave?

It is a popular problem for many business owners. The issue is not specific to or plagues anyone nation; it is a global plague that siphons off billions of dollars and impacts small as well as larger businesses. In the United States, companies experience over $40 billion in losses annually. Employees steal items such as co-workers' belongings, computer equipment, toilet paper, band-aids, and confidential files. Office theft can be committed by anyone, including auxiliary staff to managers. Three factors affect whether an individual employee steal. They are personal integrity, situational pressures, or opportunity. Companies can use various strategies to minimize or eliminate this problem, from pre-employment screening to simply educating your workers about the problem.

Occupational theft is a billion-dollar industry in and of itself. Every year global industries face the challenge of minimising the loss of inventory, goods, and financial standing. Numerous measures have been implemented but with the onset of the global financial recession, people have become even more desperate and innovative in their methods to siphon off company funds.

Companies are even more devastated by the fact that loyalty cannot be bought as those who are guiltier of such violations, are those who have worked with these businesses for years. As such, employee theft would have been going on for many years before the thief is exposed. Hundreds of thousands to millions of dollars will remain lost and, in many cases, the damage would be permanent.

For this reason, companies cannot believe that they are invincible to fraud and employee theft. Security measures must be implemented. Anti-theft policies should be drafted and disseminated to every worker. Businesses must work diligently to engender great employee morale. Finally, perpetrators who are caught must be prosecuted publicly, so that others are deterred. Only in doing so the present upward trend will be levelled off.

The study included in this book has sought to identify the occurrence of office theft in a multi-disciplinary tertiary institution in Jamaica. After conducting a literature review utilising several internet journals, recommendations were offered based on the results from the questionnaire. These recommendations included that the organisation clearly and repeatedly communicate the strategies and policies for security and safety. This allows employees to become more aware and proactive about securing their belongings and preventing instances of office theft.

References

(2000). *Attendance Management - working together: Guidelines for Absenteeism Control.* http://www.benefits.org/interface/cost/absent2.htm

(2001). *Combating absenteeism, employer-employee.com.* http://www.employer-employee.com/absent.html

(2001). *Investigating workplace theft: Sherlock.* http://www.bankersonline.com/security/gurus_sec01e.html

(2005). *Employee motivation, the organisational environment and productivity.* Accel Team. http://www.accel-team.com/human_relations/hrels_06_mcclelland.html

American Heritage Dictionary, (2006). *Definitions of absenteeism.* http://www.ask.com/web?q=what+is++absenteeism&qsrc=1&o=0

Bacas, H., (1987). *To stop a thief - employee theft; includes related articles on reducing theft and on time-theft.* http://findarticles.com/p/articles/mi_m 1154/is_v75/ai_4963240

Bachman, R., (1994). *Crime data brief: Violence and theft in the workplace.* http://www.ojp.usdoj.gov/bjs/pub/pdf/ thefwork.pdf

Brodsky, N., (2002). *Street smarts: The unkindest cut of all.* Inc. Magazine. http://www.inc.com/magazine/2002100 1/24698_Printer_Friendly.html

Brown, D., (2003). *Career Information, Career Counselling, and Career Development* (8th Ed.) Boston, Allyn and Bacon.

Eisenberg, B., Johnson, L., (2001). *Being honest about being dishonest.* CareerJournal.com, The Wall Street Journal. http://www.careerjournal.com/hrcenter/

shrm/papers/20011022-shrm-white-eisenberg.html

Fenn, D., (1995). *Workplace theft: Preventing employee pilferage.* http://www.inc.com/magazine/19950201/2158_Printer_Friendly.html

Fisher, A., (2015). *U.S. retail workers are No. 1...in employee theft.* Fortune.com. http://fortune.com/2015/01/26/us-retail-worker-theft/

Helps, HG., (2012, May 20). *More fraud! Complaints valued at over $2b filed in last 3 yrs.* The Jamaica Gleaner. Retrieved from http://www.jamaicaobserver.com/news/More-fraud--Complaints-valued-at-over--2b-filed-in-last-3-yrs_11507801

Henry, J., (1997). *How to stop employee theft.* http://www.truckstoptravelplaza.com/1997/n2/028a97n2.html

Jacoby, N., (1999). *Battling workplace theft: Sometimes the most loyal employees are the*

biggest thieves.
http://money.cnn.com/1999/08/19/inve
sting/q_employeetheft/

Klein, H., (2014). *Occupational Fraud – Still a big issue for business.*
http://www.eisneramper.com/Trends_an
d_Developments/Fraud-Employee-Theft-
0214.aspx

Lasky, S., (2013, June 20). *Growing internal employee theft crisis creates havoc for major retailers.*
http://www.securityinfowatch.com/articl
e/10964917/jack-l-hayes-internationals-
annual-retail-theft-survey-shows-
disturbing-trend-of-internal-employee-
theft

Lee, M., (2000). *Incentive programs can do wonders for office morale.* Puget Sound Business Journal (Seattle).
http://seattle.bizjournals.com/seattle/sto
ries/2000/07/31/smallb3.html

Nowak, M., (1997). *Arresting employee theft.*
http://money.cnn.com/1997/11/13/smb
usiness/theft_a/

Reid, T., (2012, July 15). *Identity Theft Hits Prison
Service.* The Jamaica Gleaner.
http://jamaica-
gleaner.com/gleaner/20120715/news/ne
ws1.html

Roche, J., (2006). *An HR manager's guide to
employee assistance programs.* The Wall
Street Journal.
http://www.careerjournal.com/hrcenter/
ipma/20060825-ipma.html

Stirn, M., (2014, November 10). *Financial and
Internal Control Whitepaper – Part 1.*
http://stirnconsulting.biz/2014/11/10/fi
nancial-and-internal-control-whitepaper-
part-1/

Sullivan, J., (2006). *Thirty-eight percent of managers
say they have fired someone for stealing at the
office, careerbuilder.com's survey finds.*

http://www.careerbuilder.com/share/ab
outus/pressreleasesdetail.aspx?siteid=cbp
r321&id=pr321&ed=12%2f31%2f2006&sd=
8%2f22%2f2006&sc_cmp1=cb_pr321_&cbR
ecursionCnt=1&cbsid=bc0f7f1fcc5947798bf
ab8467fb3d879-243612911-TH-4

Taylor, L., (2006). *Four in 10 managers have fired
employees for theft.*
http://www.inc.com/news/articles/2006
09/theft.html?partner=rss

ABOUT THE AUTHOR

Denise N. Fyffe, Dip. SD, B.Sc., PGDip.Ed., pursuing M.Ed., b.1981 from Kingston, Jamaica. Since 2001, she has worked in Education and Training, Publishing, and Information Technology. During her career, she partnered with several organizations including Infoserv Institute of Technology, Heart Trust NTA, Pearson Education, University College of the Caribbean, and Prometric.

In addition to studying Software Development and Design offered from the

Caribbean Institute of Technology, she completed her Bachelor of Science degree in Career Development and Counselling at the Vocational Training and Development Institute. Presently, she holds a Post Graduate Diploma in Education and is pursuing a Master of Education degree. As a child, she attended Harbour View Primary and Camperdown High. Denise holds fast to the philosophy that you should follow your interests as knowledge empowers you and does not set limitations on your potential.

For over a decade Denise has authored over 30 books. Denise believes her true calling in life is to be a writer and all else are bonus gifts that she has the freedom to explore. Her morals are deeply rooted in Christian principles and she lives to be a genuine example of her faith.

RECOMMENDED BOOKS

The Expert Teacher's Guide on How to Motivate Students

The book explains who an expert teacher is and how to become one. Then it delves into how to get students to learn any subject by implementing effective motivation strategies.

The Guidance Counsellor's Handbook

This book highlights the psychometric movement, the trait, and factor theory as well as legislation that impacted the development of present guidelines and ethical standards. It also looks at the roles and responsibilities of a counselor.

The Jamaican Guidance Counsellor's Handbook

This handbook briefly introduces the Jamaican educational system. It also examines the various roles and responsibilities of a Jamaican Guidance Counsellor.

Thieves in the Workplace

Occupational theft is a billion-dollar industry. Numerous measures are implemented but with the global financial recession, people have become more desperate and innovative in their methods to siphon off company funds.

The Philosophy of Education and Work

This book provides an outlook as to how Philosophy investigates the all-important question of how education and work influence elements in modern society, how they are impacted by other factors such as gender.

Empowering the 21st Century Worker

This book explores the analysis, implications, and findings of on-the-job training. It takes a close look at the processes and infrastructure in place for employee training and whether a positive organizational change is a result.

Learning Management System Efficiency vs. Staff Proficiency

This book examines the level of staff proficiency with the Learning Management System and the resulting impact on student satisfaction and attrition levels, within a particular learning organization.

Examining Career Development and Australia

This book examines the career development strategies implemented in both Australia and Jamaica to augment the conditions brought on by both global change and crisis. It highlights the social and economic transformation in Australia.

Is the Registry Happy: Examining Career Development within Learning Organizations

This book analyses career development strategies being implemented at learning organizations.

Sophie's Place: Examining Career Development for the Disabled

This book examines the career development strategies implemented at Sophie's Place for the disabled. It highlights the physical, social, and cognitive limitations of the children who live there.

All books are available at online bookstores, including Lulu.com and Amazon.com.

DEAR READER

Thank you for reading this book.

It means so much that you have taken the time out of your busy schedule. Nothing makes us happier than knowing that someone is reading, and hopefully enjoying, what took us many months, even years, to create.

Please stay with us on this journey. We need your feedback, opinions, and guidance about the book. We would appreciate a few lines of review on Amazon:

http://www.amazon.com

You can also write us a note at Jamaica Pen Publishing on Facebook, or Twitter and at The Island Journal website.

Again, thank you.